LINKING THE PAST AND PRESENT

WHAT DID THE
ANCIENT
GREEKS
DO FOR ME?

Patrick Catel

Heinemann Library
Chicago, Illinois

www.heinemannraintree.com
Visit our website to find out
more information about
Heinemann-Raintree books.

To order:
☎ Phone 888-454-2279
🖥 Visit www.heinemannraintree.com
to browse our catalog and order online.

Edited by Megan Cotugno and Laura Knowles
Designed by Richard Parker
Original illustrations © Capstone Global Library Limited 2010
Illustrated by Roger@KJA-artists.com
Picture research by Hannah Taylor
Originated by Capstone Global Library Limited
Printed and bound in China by CTPS

14 13 12 11 10
10 9 8 7 6 5 4 3 2
ISBN 13: 9781432937461 / ISBN 10: 1432937464 (hardcover)

Library of Congress Cataloging-in-Publication Data
Catel, Patrick.
  What did the ancient Greeks do for me? / Patrick Catel.
    p. cm. -- (Linking the past and present)
  Includes bibliographical references and index.
  ISBN 978-1-4329-3746-1 (hc) -- ISBN 978-1-4329-3753-9
(pb) 1. Greece--Civilization--To 146 B.C.--Juvenile literature.
2. Civilization, Modern--Greek influences--Juvenile literature.
I. Title.
  DF77.C385 2011
  938--dc22

                    2009039670

Acknowledgments
The author and publisher are grateful to the following for
permission to reproduce copyright material: akg-images
p. **19** (©Walt Disney Pictures/Album); Alamy Images p. **25**
(©David Gee 5); The Art Archive p. **20** (Museo Nazionale
Romano Rome/Dagli Orti); Corbis pp. **9** (Gianni Dagli Orti),
27 (epa/Kim Ludbrook); Getty Images p. **21** (AFP Photo/
Fabrice Coffrini); istockphoto p. **11** (©narvikk); Photolibrary
pp. **6** (Marco Simoni), **13** (Tony Savino), **15** (Stocktrek
Corporation), **17** (Britain on View/David Hunter), **23** (Peter &
Georgina Bowater).

Cover photograph of the Parthenon, Athens, Greece,
reproduced with permission of istockphoto/©Ricardo
De Mattos.

We would like to thank Dr. Andrew Bayliss for his invaluable
help in the preparation of this book.

Every effort has been made to contact copyright holders
of any material reproduced in this book. Any omissions
will be rectified in subsequent printings if notice is given
to the publisher.

All the Internet addresses (URLs) given in this book were valid
at the time of going to press. However, due to the dynamic
nature of the Internet, some addresses may have changed, or
sites may have changed or ceased to exist since publication.
While the author and publisher regret any inconvenience this
may cause readers, no responsibility for any such changes can
be accepted by either the author or the publisher.

Contents

Look for the Then and Now boxes. They highlight parts of ancient Greek culture that are present in our modern world.

Any words appearing in the text in bold, **like this**, are explained in the glossary.

What Did the Ancient Greeks Do for Me?

Our modern world owes a lot to the ancient Greeks. Do you have a favorite movie or play? Perhaps you have marveled at the fantastic giants and other creatures in stories such as *Harry Potter*? Do you love watching the amazing athletes in the Olympic Games? You can't vote yet, but do you ever think about how lucky we are to live in a society where we choose our leaders?

The ancient Greeks are to thank for these ideas and inventions, and many more. We see their influence in many of our buildings. When political elections come around, we can thank the ancient Greeks for inventing the idea of **democracy**. Ancient Greek technology, science, and philosophy continue to influence our daily lives and the modern world.

You might be surprised to find out some of the things modern armies have in common with ancient Greek soldiers.

The Parthenon was an important temple in ancient Greece. Does it remind you of any modern buildings you have visited?

Who Were the Ancient Greeks?

Ancient Greece was made up of the Balkan Peninsula and hundreds of islands in the northeastern Mediterranean Sea. Three-quarters of Greece's land surface is mountains. Most cities were built near the coast, where the ancient Greeks could find food in the sea and travel easily using boats.

With such a long coastline and so many islands, the sea was very important for ancient Greek culture. Early Greeks sailed the Mediterranean Sea and traded with other people in the area, including the ancient Egyptians. They also took control of areas around the Mediterranean. This meant Greek culture spread across the ancient world. When Greece became part of the Roman Empire in 146 BCE, the Romans copied Greek ideas and art.

The Parthenon was built in Athens during the years 447–432 BCE. With its size, beautiful architecture, and detailed carvings, the Parthenon represents the height of Athenian culture.

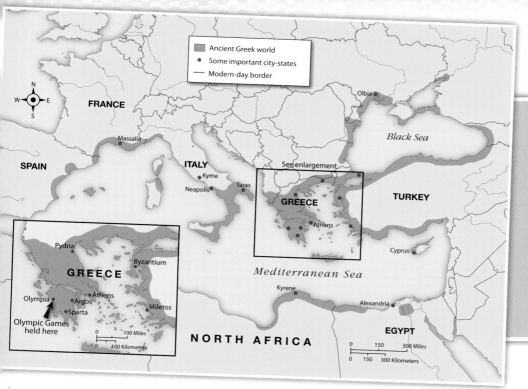

This map shows ancient Greece and the lands it controlled. Most ancient Greeks lived along the coast or on islands. They traveled and traded around the Mediterranean Sea.

City-states

Ancient Greece was actually a group of **city-states** with shared customs. These city-states were sometimes at peace with one another, but they were also often at war. The two most powerful and famous city-states were Athens and Sparta. They were bitter rivals at times and eventually fought a long war called the Peloponnesian War (431–404 BCE). At the end of the war, Sparta forced Athens to tear down its defensive walls, making it much less powerful.

Before the Peloponnesian War, the ancient Greeks managed to band together to fight off invasions from the powerful Persian Empire (modern-day Iran), in 490 BCE and 480–479 BCE. The Classical Period (479–323 BCE) began following the defeat of the Persians. Most of the greatest philosophers, healers, and leaders of ancient Greece lived at this time, and the knowledge they wrote down is still studied today.

7

What Was Ancient Greek Art and Architecture Like?

Some of the earliest artists whose names we know today worked in ancient Greece. They painted scenes on pottery and sculpted lifelike statues of gods, heroes, and athletes. The ancient Greeks used pottery to make cups, bowls, plates, vases, jars, and just about everything else. The remains of that pottery are in museums around the world today.

Greek style

At first the Greeks only painted shapes and patterns on vases. This was during the Geometric Period (1100–750 BCE), which is also sometimes called the Dark Ages. During the Archaic Period (750–480 BCE), the Greeks began to paint characters from **myths**. By the Classical Period (479–323 BCE), the Greeks began to tell stories on pottery. Works by the artists Sophilos, the Diosphos Painter, and Kleitias are in museums today.

Sophilos

Sophilos is the first Greek vase painter in history whose name is known.

THEN...

The goal of Greek sculptors such as Phidias was to create the perfect human form. Most statues of the Archaic Period were of men striding with one foot forward. These are called *kouroi*. They did not account for the weight shift of the human body, and the forward leg was longer than the back leg. By the Classical Period, the Greeks had mastered the human form and understood how the body shifted with movement.

This is a Roman copy of the Greek statue *Diskobolos*, from the Classical Period. The lifelike sculpture shows an athlete getting ready to throw a discus.

...NOW

The ancient Greeks were the first to create the perfect human form in their sculptures. Later, European artists rediscovered and carried on that knowledge. Today, artists create realistic sculptures, like the Greeks in ancient times, to commemorate famous heroes, politicians, and scholars. However, art has developed even further and continues to change, with new ideas and ways of doing things.

The Parthenon

The Parthenon is the most famous ancient Greek temple. It sits on top of the **Acropolis** in Athens and was completed in 432 BCE, during the Classical Period. What is called the "classical style" of architecture today is modeled on the Parthenon.

Some modern buildings look similar to the gray-and-white ruins found in Greece today. In ancient times, however, temples were actually painted in bright colors.

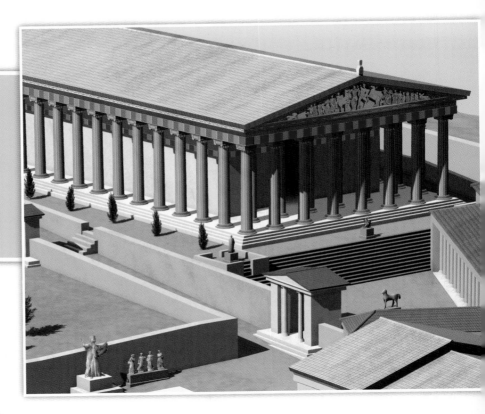

THEN...

The ancient Greeks understood **optical illusion**. Their temples had columns that could support huge stone roofs. To the human eye, the straight lines of the columns could look bent outward from a distance. The ancient Greeks made the columns of the Parthenon lean slightly inward, which made them look perfectly straight!

The Parthenon was the temple of Athena, the goddess of Athens. Inside was a 12-meter- (40-foot-) tall statue of Athena by the artist Phidias. He made many other sculptures in ancient Greece, including the statue of the god Zeus inside the Temple of Zeus at Olympia. This statue was one of the seven wonders of the ancient world.

The Lincoln Memorial in Washington, D.C., was built in the style of an ancient Greek temple. Visitors can imagine what it must have been like to enter a grand temple such as the Parthenon.

...NOW

Everywhere we look it is easy to see that modern buildings owe a lot to the Greeks. The Lincoln Memorial in Washington, D.C., for example, looks like an ancient Greek temple. The British Museum in London also looks very much like an ancient Greek temple. It also has the original sculptures of the Parthenon in its collection.

What Did the Ancient Greeks Believe?

Myths and stories played an important part in ancient Greek life. People **worshipped** many gods, whom they believed could influence their lives. Priests and priestesses guarded the temples. They also held sacrifices, rituals, and festivals. The ancient Greeks celebrated many festivals. In Athens, there were festivals on almost half the days of the year!

Gods and goddesses

The Greeks made offerings of food, drink, animals, and other objects to please the gods. Zeus was ruler of the gods, and Hera was his wife. Apollo was the god of music and healing, Ares was the god of war, and Poseidon was the god of the seas. Athena was the goddess of war and wisdom, and Aphrodite was the goddess of love. There were many other gods and god-like heroes.

Nike

Athena Nike was the goddess of victory. You can probably recognize the name "Nike" from a famous brand name of today.

THEN...

There were many monstrous creatures in ancient Greek myths. The centaur had the bottom half of a horse and the top half of a man. The griffin had the head and wings of an eagle and the body of a lion. The Titans were the gods who ruled over Earth before Zeus defeated them.

This statue in New York City represents Atlas, the ancient Greek Titan who was forced to hold up the heavens on his shoulders.

People no longer worship the gods of ancient Greece, but we still remember them. Many things in the world around us have been named after ancient Greek gods, heroes, and monsters. For example, the groups of stars known as Orion and Scorpius are named for Orion the hunter and the scorpion who stung him.

How Did the Ancient Greeks Fight?

The ancient Greeks had well-trained armies and navies. They also invented new weapons and ways of fighting. In their war against the mighty Persian Empire they were able to defeat a much bigger army because of their methods, weapons, and training.

Sparta

The ancient Greek **city-state** of Sparta created the ultimate soldiers. Every male Spartan was taken from his mother at the age of seven and sent to live in a military camp. He lived there until he was 30 years old. He was taught fighting, discipline, athletics, and how to endure pain. After 13 years of training, he became a Spartan soldier.

A Spartan life

The simple, disciplined life of a Spartan soldier gave us the saying a "Spartan existence," which means a very simple lifestyle.

THEN...

Foot soldiers in ancient Greece were called hoplites, named after the round hoplon shields they used. Hoplites fought shoulder to shoulder in a line called a phalanx. Each shield covered the exposed area of the man to the left, creating a wall of shields. The hoplites wore helmets, **breastplates**, and **greaves** to protect their bodies. They fought with spears and swords.

Modern-day weapons such as tanks and projectile launchers are similar to the ancient Greek catapult and crossbow. They are able to fire on enemies at a distance, so that the soldiers are further from danger.

...NOW

Warfare is still a fact of modern life. Military training, methods, and weapons have become more advanced through the ages. However, the ancient Greek example shows us how strategy, training, and technology led to a stronger army that could defeat greater numbers. In fact, the word "strategy" comes from the Greek word *strategos*, which means "a general."

What Sports Did the Ancient Greeks Play?

Ancient Greek sporting events were usually held in honor of the gods. Popular sports included wrestling, running, long jump, boxing, discus and javelin throwing, and horse and chariot racing. The most famous of ancient Greece's athletic events was the Olympic Festival. It was held in Olympia every four years in honor of the god Zeus.

Gymnasiums and palaestras

Every ancient Greek **city-state** had a public gymnasium, where people exercised and socialized. They also had a wrestling school called a *palaestra* where people could learn a sport called *pankration*. This was a cross between wrestling and boxing. Anything except biting or gouging out eyes was allowed in this fighting event. Men died during the fights—sometimes because they refused to give up.

Spartan athletes

Many Spartan soldiers were also Olympic athletes. They were well prepared for competing and winning because of all the difficult training they did.

THEN...

The prize in the ancient Greek Olympic Games was a simple crown of olive leaves. However, athletes were treated like heroes in their own city-states. They were given parades, money, and even had sculptures built in their honor. Only Greek men who were not slaves could take part in the games, and women were not even allowed to watch.

Ancient Greek Olympians were famous around the ancient world. Many athletes today are famous worldwide. Some, such as boxing champion Randolph Turpin (right), even have statues made in their honor.

...NOW

The Olympic Games were restarted in modern times and have become an important international event. Women take part and are just as admired and respected as the men. Olympic athletes are still treated like heroes in their own countries and around the world.

How Did the Ancient Greeks Invent Theater?

A storyteller named Homer created the *Iliad* and the *Odyssey*. These are long poems that were often spoken out loud to audiences. They are called epic poems. The *Iliad* is about the hero Achilles and the Trojan War, which was a famous war against the city of Troy. The *Odyssey* is about the travels of the hero Odysseus. The ancient Greeks passed on the stories of their gods and heroes through these epic poems, as well as through songs and music. When actors with speaking parts were added to the performances, theater was born.

This picture shows what an ancient Greek theater such as the one at Epidaurus would have looked like. Some ancient Greek theaters are still used for performances today.

THEN...

In ancient Greece, plays competed for prizes at festivals, much like film festivals in modern times. They were held in large, open-air theaters. The audience sat in rows of stone benches, arranged in a semicircle. The shape of the theater made sound travel well. This meant a person in the back row could still easily hear the action on stage. An architect named Polyclitus the Younger was famous for his theater at Epidaurus, which could seat 14,000 people.

Tragedy and comedy

Ancient Greek playwrights wrote tragedies and comedies to be performed for audiences at festivals around Greece. Most of the originals of these works are lost or were destroyed by early Christians. Tragedies by Aeschylus, Sophocles, and Euripides survive. Only 11 complete comedies from the same period survive, all of them by Aristophanes.

Walt Disney Pictures
presenta
HERCULES

The stories of the ancient Greeks are still told in plays and movies today. Hercules, shown here as a Disney character, is one of the most famous heroes of Greek legend.

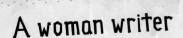

A woman writer

Sappho of Lesbos is the most famous of only a few women known to have written poetry in ancient Greece.

...NOW

The English playwright William Shakespeare carried on the Greek tradition many years later with his own comedies and tragedies. Some ancient Greek plays are still performed today, and the stories of the ancient Greeks are popular subjects in modern movies. Even the architecture and acoustics of modern theaters, for both stage and movies, owe a lot to the ancient Greeks.

Who Were the Ancient Greek Philosophers?

The ancient Greeks used philosophy to explore ideas and questions. Philosophy was important because it used **observation** and clear thinking to understand the world. The ancient Greeks believed in their gods, but they also tried to figure out ideas and problems for themselves. These ancient beliefs in observation still form the basis of modern science.

Socrates, Plato, and Aristotle

Socrates, Plato, and Aristotle are the three most famous philosophers of ancient Athens. Socrates believed in asking questions in order to learn more about life. Plato was his student. Plato founded the Academy in Athens, where Aristotle was his student. Aristotle went on to become a teacher at the Academy. He believed that every subject could be understood through **logic**.

This is a Roman copy of a Greek sculpture of Aristotle, who shaped the way people thought for hundreds of years.

THEN...

Athens was a rich and **democratic city-state**, with wealthy and educated citizens who had time to develop ideas. However, ancient Greek city-states were far from perfect. There were many slaves, who had few rights. And women were far from equal in Greek society. Despite this, ancient Greek philosophy had a lasting influence and has been studied and debated ever since.

Philosophy

The word "philosophy" is made up of two Greek words. *Philia* means "love of" and *sophia* means "wisdom."

Scientists at the world's largest particle collider in Switzerland are trying to discover how our universe began. They are using the ancient Greek idea of observing the world in order to learn about it.

...NOW

Modern science carries on the ideas of human observation invented by the ancient Greeks. Scientific study has brought us closer to understanding our world and even our universe. Students at universities around the world are still required to read the works of the famous Greek philosophers. Many universities offer degrees in philosophy. However, conditions are more equal today. Both men and women from a variety of backgrounds study philosophy at these universities.

What Did the Ancient Greeks Do for Science?

The ancient Greeks came up with many scientific ideas that we still use today, in the fields of mathematics, astronomy, and medicine.

Pure mathematics

One branch of mathematics is called pure mathematics because it is the study of numbers, amounts, and space for their own sake. The ancient Greeks were the first people to practice this science. For them, it was a way to observe the world. Euclid and Pythagoras, two ancient Greek mathematicians, discovered ideas in **geometry** and **algebra** that are still used today.

When Heron made his steam engine, he did not realize how useful steam could be for creating power and doing work.

THEN...

Greek scholars used their mathematical talents to create marvelous inventions. Heron (c. 10–70 CE) was a Greek mathematician and engineer living in Alexandria (see map on page 7). He created the world's first simple steam engine. A pot was filled with water and placed over a fire. Two tubes let steam flow into a ball made of metal. The ball had two curved tubes that vented steam, which then made the ball rotate. Heron thought the device was a fun toy.

Astronomy

Astronomy is the study of the stars and their movements. The ancient Greeks named the brightest moving lights they could see *planetes*, which is where our word "planet" comes from. Pythagoras studied astronomy as well as mathematics. He is thought to be the first person to figure out that Earth is round. He did this more than 2,500 years ago.

Anaxagoras, another ancient Greek astronomer, was the first to realize that the moon does not give off its own light, but rather reflects the light from the sun. Aristarchus of Samos was the first to say that Earth moves around the sun.

Almost 2,000 years after Heron's time, we now use the power of steam in generators such as this to create electricity for homes and businesses.

...NOW

Heron was ahead of his time, but he did not see the steam engine's possible use for work. Hundreds of years later, the power of steam was used in new machines. It was very important in the **Industrial Revolution** of the late 1700s and early 1800s. More and more steam-powered machines were built. Even today, most power plants around the world produce electricity using steam power.

Tools

Archimedes was a Greek mathematician. He was the first to describe the **lever** as a tool, and he also invented the **pulley**. Both these tools allowed people to lift heavy weights easily, which was very important for building structures. Archimedes was also known for the military machines he invented.

Medicine

Asclepius was a mythical ancient Greek healer and son of the god Apollo. He was so skilled at healing that he was made a god. His symbol was a serpent wrapped around a staff, which is similar to a rod or walking stick. A similar image is used today as a symbol of healing. Hippocrates is known as the father of medicine. He was one of the first healers to use the physical examination of patients as the way he decided what was wrong with them. The beliefs of Hippocrates are the basis of the **Hippocratic oath**, which doctors still follow today.

Vending machines

The ancient Greeks built the first vending machines! They were used in temples. In return for a coin, you could receive a small amount of holy water.

THEN...

Archimedes invented a screw that was so helpful that it is still used today. It is called the Archimedes screw in his honor. Archimedes placed a screw inside a hollow tube. This could be turned by hand or by a windmill. As it turned, the screw could transfer water from one place to another.

This modern water screw uses the same idea as Archimedes' screw did over 2,000 years ago. It is a simple machine that moves water upward to help drain farmland in the Netherlands.

...NOW

Archimedes' original design has hardly changed at all in over 2,000 years. It is still used around the world for watering crops, preventing flooding, and transferring water from place to place. Today, people also use another, very similar type of screw, called a screw conveyor, that is used to push dry material upward.

What Was Ancient Greek Democracy?

Each **city-state** in ancient Greece had its own kind of government. At first, Athens was ruled by kings. They were later replaced by a small group of the city's wealthiest men. This system of government is known as an **oligarchy**. Sometimes a single **tyrant** would try to take control from this group. The oligarchies were often so bad that people would welcome a tyrant!

Solon and Cleisthenes

In 594 BCE, there was a lot of unrest in Athens. Thousands of poor people had been forced into debt and had to sell themselves into slavery. The people chose a leader named Solon to try to solve the problems. Solon got rid of the laws that allowed people to sell themselves into slavery to repay debts. He then created a government in which all Athenian citizens could have their say. Later, in 508 BCE, a man named Cleisthenes further established **democracy** in Athens. He is known as the "father of democracy."

THEN...

Ancient Athens created the first democracy in which people did not have to be rich in order to take part. However, people did have to be citizens. A citizen was a free, adult man who had been born in Athens. Slaves and women were not counted as citizens and were not allowed to vote or join the government.

This woman is voting in an election in South Africa to decide who will be the next president.

...NOW

Today, there are democracies all around the world in which all adults, no matter their sex, race, background, or beliefs, can stand for election as well as vote. It took a long time to get to this point. Women in the United States did not have the right to vote until more than 2,500 years after Solon's first Athenian democracy.

Key Dates

Here is an outline of important moments in the history and culture of ancient Greece:

3000–1100 BCE   **The Bronze Age**
around 1200 BCE   The Trojan War takes place

900–750 BCE   **The Geometric Period**
around 900 BCE   The Greek alphabet is invented

around 900 BCE   Geometric-patterned pottery is created

776 BCE   The first Olympic Games are held

around 750 BCE   Homer creates the *Iliad* and the *Odyssey* stories

750–480 BCE   **The Archaic Period**
590s BCE   Solon gets rid of the old, harsh laws in Athens

500s BCE   Pythagoras develops his mathematical ideas

508 BCE   **Democracy** begins in Athens

490 BCE   Greeks defeat Persians at the Battle of Marathon

479–323 BCE	**The Classical Period**
	During this period, theater thrives in Athens. Socrates, Plato, and Aristotle develop Greek philosophy.
around 460–430 BCE	The Greek sculptor Phidias creates his works
447–432 BCE	The Parthenon is built
around 400 BCE	Hippocrates practices scientific medicine
431–404 BCE	The Peloponnesian War takes place. Sparta is victorious over Athens.
338 BCE	Philip of Macedonia takes control of Greece
336–31 BCE	**The Hellenistic Period**
336–323 BCE	Alexander the Great, son of Philip of Macedonia, conquers many lands
200s BCE	Archimedes creates the Archimedes screw and other inventions
146 BCE	Rome conquers Greece, making it part of the Roman Empire
after 146 BCE	Greek scientists and mathematicians, such as Heron, continue to work and invent things for the Romans

Glossary

Acropolis ancient fortress built on a high hill in the center of a city. In Athens, the Parthenon and other important buildings and temples were built on the Acropolis.

algebra type of mathematics that uses letters and symbols for numbers

BCE short for "Before the Common Era." BCE is used for all the years before year 1.

breastplate protective armor worn over the chest during battle

city-state self-governing state made up of a city and the land around it

democracy system of government in which every citizen can vote and elect officials. A country is called democratic if it uses this system of government.

geometry type of mathematics that studies angles, shapes, and lines

greaves piece of armor covering the lower leg

Hippocratic oath promise made by doctors that they will follow the principles of medicine and respect and treat patients the best they can

Industrial Revolution period in the 1700s and 1800s in Europe and North America when new machines were invented for work and large factories were set up

lever long, thin object used as a tool to lift something heavy by putting one end under that thing and pushing the other end down

logic way of thinking based on sensible reasons for doing something

myth story about gods and heroes from ancient times

observation looking at something in detail

oligarchy when a country is run by a small group of people

optical illusion image that tricks your eyes and makes you see something that is not really there

pulley tool that is a wheel with a rope or chain over it, where one end is pulled to lift something heavy on the other end

tyrant cruel leader who seizes power without having a right to it

worship praising and showing respect for a god or gods. It may involve singing, praying, and other ways of showing respect.

Find Out More

Books

Owens, Greg. *Hands-on Ancient History: The History and Activities of the Ancient Greeks.* Chicago: Heinemann Library, 2007.

Pearson, Anne. *Eyewitness: Ancient Greece.* New York: Dorling Kindersley, 2007.

Rice, Rob S. *Ancient Warfare: Ancient Greek Warfare.* Pleasantville, N.Y.: Gareth Stevens, 2010.

Websites

www.socialstudiesforkids.com/subjects/ancientgreece.htm
This website has lots of information on the history of ancient Greece.

www.ancientgreece.co.uk
This website is run by the British Museum and has lots of information about ancient Greek society.

www.historyforkids.org/learn/greeks
Find out more about ancient Greek myths, sports, clothes, and much more on this useful website.

A place to visit

Metropolitan Museum of Art
1000 Fifth Avenue at 82nd Street
New York, New York 10028-0198
(212) 535-7710
www.metmuseum.org

Index